Household Gods

poems

Bonnie Proudfoot

ISBN: 979-8-9855242-3-9

Sheila-Na-Gig Editions
Russell, KY
Hayley Mitchell Haugen, Editor
www.sheilanagigblog.com

Acknowledgments

This book would not have been possible without the faith and guidance of kind friends, including the mentorship of Pauletta Hansel and students in the Draft to Craft classes, the Every Tuesday (more or less) Poetry Group, including Wendy McVicker, Deni Naffziger, Jane Ann Fuller, Jean Mikhail, Molly Schoenhopf, Kristine Williams, and a special thanks to Dan Canterbury and Andy Semons. Thanks also to Hayley Mitchell Haugen and Sheila-Na-Gig Editions for supporting this book. You all bring the light.

I am grateful to the following journals and organizations for previously publishing or honoring versions of these poems:

Change Seven: "Mimosa"
Gyroscope Review: "El Tiempo," "For Christopher Robin"
JMWW: "Jetstar 88"
New Ohio Review (online edition): "Superpowers"
Northern Appalachia Review: "Control"
Ohio Poetry Association — First Prize, Ides of March contest: "Back from Aqueduct"
Rattle, Poets Respond: "Sweet Forgiveness"
Sheila-Na-Gig online: "Broken Moon," "Throwing Like a Girl" "Bees," "What We Did"
SoFloPoJo: "Consider the Aunties and Grandmothers," "Playland"
The Laurel Review: "Household Gods"
Twelve Mile Review: "Saved"

Introduction

Bonnie Proudfoot's *Household Gods* is, first of all, an act of love. In the poem *"El Tiempo,"* the speaker reports that a woman sells poems from a streetside Spanish café: "She says the words come / from the air. The letters push into soft vellum, ink already / starting to fade" — this is a voice I trust, though not only for its candor and forthrightness. Early in the chapbook, Ralph Kramden's threatening masculinity is scored as the word rage in SCRABBLE® in the flow of an argument about the possibility of her father launching her brother to the Moon. In poem after poem, we see lived life. As such, anger and rage infuse this work — Joy does make a welcome appearance in the next poem, "Sweet Forgiveness": "and the cantor sang / so rich and deep, a voice that sounded like, well, / pot roast with gravy, and then the *shofar* rang out, / held us in a power so great it felt like dark giving way...". Sin and forgiveness play peek-a-boo throughout. And in the poem "Elegy for Kitty Genovese" we hear it comes down to this: "What if to speak means to open a wound, a knot of rage and grief?" Later, in "Back from Aqueduct," Proudfoot describes Womankind in its complicated commonplaceness:

and, I can say it now, what is not lost and can't be ignored
is how every bright pan, every spotless counter, was more
than a tactical gamble, it was a vanguard against sin,
a wager against darkness, a bet she needed to win.

If this chapbook is a description of America with its racetracks and religion and racism, it's a description written in the suffering and the head-thrown-back laughter of men and women:

and when we looked toward the east
we could almost see the elevated train,
the Jamaica Avenue line, and beyond that, Rockaway,
the ocean and forever, and we could turn the radio up

as loud as we wanted, this house of the rising sun,
this sun that burned through the thin distant haze,
and we spread dirty sheets on that sullied ground,
and after making art, we looked at the sky.

—Roy Bentley, author of *My Mother's Red Ford:*
New & Selected (1986-2020)

For Anna, Shirley, Steve, and Mugsie,
the *Lares and Penates,*
and for Wren

"... you are everywhere, source
of wisdom and anguish... "
—Louise Glück, *The Wild Iris*

Contents

El Tiempo

In Madrid, minibikes weave up narrow blocks,
grates over shop doorways unlock around 2-ish,

we pace ourselves, my aunt, my cousin, me,
reset our clock. We are three generations,

a distance that disappears viewing Goya, El Greco.
Imagine an ocean passage, Ellis Island, Brooklyn,

then Queens, everyone within inches. Grief and strife
pierce apartment walls, thread into the bloodline.

"If anyone asks what you are," my mother instructs,
"tell them you are American." I try. Strangers

see right through that gambit. My mother dies
at 64, just before my cousin is born, this cousin

whose fingers swell and throb as mine and my aunt's do,
as my mother's did. In *El Parque Retiro*, beside

the Crystal Palace, a dark-haired woman sits
at a folding table with a Royal typewriter.

"Give me a theme, and I will give you a poem,"
her poster promises. *"El tiempo,"* I say. Time.

The matter of time, she types (*en español*),
is immaterial, a bubble. Two dogs face each other

from each side of a spiral. She says the words come
from the air. The letters push into soft vellum, ink already

starting to fade. In a Barcelona café, a Flamenco dancer
spirals her veil, glances over her left shoulder. The past

is gaining ground, it's snapping at her stamping heels. We
clap faster and faster, hold tight to each other when she bows.

Superpowers

If all of my thoughts have been thought before,
who was the one who thought them? Probably
it was some stranger, but maybe not, maybe
someone I knew or maybe someone I loved so hard
that she is actually a part of me, like my grandmother,
who came by on poker nights, maybe I inhaled her
like the smoke from the tip of her Parliament, or
I ate her up like a slice of her pound cake
with lemon drizzle icing.

And superpowers? I used to think they were accidents
or destiny, like winning the lottery, or that someone could be
switched at birth, or that there could be the slightest chance
that a baby, say, me, could have hurtled to earth on
a tiny cradle-shaped spaceship from a place sort of like
Krypton, but maybe all my powers slipped in
under my bedroom door with the smoke, the smell of gin,
the pink and green neon light sifting through those slats
in the Venetian blinds, my brain soft and doughy
like warm silly putty, taking in the patterns on the wall;
sometimes everything is pink, and sometimes everything
tastes like lemon, sometimes the soundtrack
in my head is the overture to *Guys and Dolls*,
and what the men in the control booths who want
to learn more about brainwashing don't know
is that once you hear that overture, all you can think of
is how you can't wait to see Frank Sinatra
make his entrance as Nathan Detroit.

And of course, one day I see myself, in *my sixties*,
(for crying out loud), at my dining room table, facing
my own grown children, using some of my superpowers
to count the face cards and take tricks, to know exactly
where the line is between luck and skill, and these fingers

of mine start to fuss for an invisible cigarette, though
there is none in sight. And I know that the odds are good
that life will betray them, that their bodies will betray them,
that winning flashes off and on like a Lotto sign, and that I,
who at age six, dressed up to trick or treat as a Parliament
flip top box, all white and blue and glowing, I will
betray them, too, I who cracked open the egg
and hopped the train, and they, who filled
pickup trucks with sleeping bags and hit the road,
but for now I am here, the dealer, my elder son
on my right, thinking things like *luck be a lady,*
and *wash the cards,* thinking, *shine the bat signal,*
spin out that web, go ahead, cut 'em.

Once

upon a time, my mother told me,
a bad little boy took his little blanket
off his little bed and tied it
around his neck like Superman's cape, then
walked to his window—here
she pointed at the window in my bedroom—
he stood on the ledge and jumped out
because he thought he was Superman
and could fly

    to the moon

      Ralph Kramden
bunched up his fist and looked over the bridge
of his nose at Alice. "Just you wait 'til your father
gets home," is what I heard, not so much
about me but about my brother, the chipper
little guy never quite seemed to fit, as if a smack
could slap somebody straight or keep him
from trying to protect his mother, which was not
a bad thought,

    tough luck,

      the fist will find you
in every corner, the belt about to be taken off
the pants, Grandma from across the street, peering
over her glasses. In Scrabble, R is one point,
A is one point, G is two points and E is one point;
it's only a five-point word, so small
but it fits in everywhere on the board, can be attached
so easily to the other words. Maybe what I want
to say is that the moon seems so serene and beautiful
when you look at it from far away but who knows
it might have an apartment with a kid looking
back out at me thinking
she could fly.

Sweet Forgiveness

All day in temple we listened to the rabbi
intone in Hebrew, his voice a dedicated
monotone, broken mostly by standing, sitting,
then standing, each time my father's hand
on my shoulder, his stomach grumbling next to me,
hopefully God wasn't noticing me noticing
my dad's bad breath, and the fact that he was
just kind of mumbling along, didn't seem to know
the actual words to the prayers, and we were
fasting to atone, intentionally supposed to apologize
to others we needed to seek forgiveness from,
and I knew sometimes I did not include
my little brother (but come on), or I did not offer
to set the table, get my nose out of a book
and get up and help out of my own accord,
think of my poor mother on her feet all day,
and the cantor sang so rich and deep,
a voice that sounded like, well, pot roast with gravy,
and then the *shofar* rang out, held us
in a power so great it felt like dark giving way
to light. And finally home where the table
had already been set like an act of forgiveness,
food with incantatory names, *kreplach, schmaltz herring,
kishke, challah*. None of this food, like sweet forgiveness itself,
could ever be bought, it had to be touched
by the hands of those who cared for us, served when it
was most needed, waited for, earned.

For Christopher Robin

Thanks for sending me that photo
of our trip out west, Grandma's hair
in curlers, peeking out the camper door,
your forehead almost reaching my chin.
Home, reading *Winnie the Pooh*
by flashlight, our knees made a puptent
from the blanket. Through the walls,
Mom did dishes. Dad's jaw did not
unclench. We had pockets stuffed
with secrets. How else could we
get by? We always needed to ask
permission. You loved Eeyore,
mourned his missing tail. I loved
the Hundred Aker Wood, so huge,
tiny sets of tracks heading somewhere,
like they knew which way to go.

Saved
(after Camille Dungy)

"Its useless nature itself is the reason to admire it" —Basho

This poker and dawdler, this dollop of perpetual contemplation, this pencil
twirler, finger-weaver, finger up nose, fingers in ears, finger in navel, audience
of one, this knot of perplexity, molehill of monkey business, detour finder,
this nick out of time, un-clocked, tunnel of undone, un-bustling, un-hustling,
deepening canyon of un, window starer, squirrel glimpser, gum popper,
stuck gum under the desk picker, out of the lines scribbler, eraser crumbler, last
in line hall-stander, punchline misser, fish tank drifter, all wishy and
flying-fishy, this *nudnik*, space cadet, out of this world, planet of separate
parts, absent that day, question dweller, syllable sounder, answer loser,
mitten loser, crayon smeller, beautiful soul, saved by the sweet, holy bell.

How many pages of photographs

do I have to flip through to get to the one
I remember her by? That one, the picture
with the roses, sitting for once in her endless
day of endless housework, that one
her hair black as a raven, streaked
with thin streamers of silver, pointy
black glasses with dots of rhinestones
that looked like they were meant for someone
who went to the beauty parlor, and I did
follow her there sometimes, waiting,
trying not to stare at ladies whose blue curls
were rolled and pinned in graceful swirls,
whose pink smocks hung loosely over pearl necklaces,
whose arms bore blue numbers that could
never be washed clean. They smoked and rasped out
dahling when they needed settings adjusted
on hairdryers, and there was *Life Magazine*,
photos of Jackie, baby Caroline, and JFK,
and who knew that soon he too would be taken,
the sorrow flowing like his death made six million
plus one killed, even though he was not Jewish,
but somehow his body too lay on those piles
to be wept over, and then came Martin Luther King,
and we all know where this is headed, Tamir Rice's
mother knows where, George Floyd's brother knows.
How does a numbered lady forgive? how does
the world recover from a river of tears that turns
into an ocean? Forgiveness knocks like a beggar.
We have so much grief to offer, but it will not find
its way in. Once my grandmother held out her arm
and I marveled at each soft wrinkle and fold,
each pink or brown mole, but now the river of tears
holds all the ashes—not another one gone,
Breonna Taylor, not again.

Consider the Aunties and Grandmothers

Points of knitting needles clicking
like daggers dicing the air,
a circle no girl wants to enter.
Born to keep the outside out,
born to wring the necks of chickens,
pound white meat into cutlets,
cream sugar into eggs, because
there are labors of love and labors
of need, labors of pain, and lifetimes
where each moment seems to click
tightly into the next, but where does
that land on a scale of suffering?
Nearsighted or farsighted, not missing
a trick, they know the wrapping paper
of success hides the bomb inside
the present. A gold ring on one hand,
a mop in the other, floors so bright
they win the Glo-Coat prize, red painted
fingernails, skeins of yarn spilling off laps,
apron pockets full of posies. When one dies,
we cover all the mirrors.

Elegy for Kitty Genovese

(i) *Scar*

If my old neighborhood is my body and P.S. 99
is my head, and the Big Park is my right hand,
then Kitty Genovese is my mouth, the train tracks
zippering through. Under streetlights, apartment units rise
behind storefronts: German deli, Turkish coffee,
Hungarian pastries, Italian pizzeria, Polish, Chinese,
Spanish spoken here, Orthodox Jews in long black coats
gossip and scold in two-hundred-year-old Yiddish.
Parents hush children and herd them indoors, spikes
driven deep from citizen spies and secret police.
In a shop window, plucked ducks and geese dangle
by their feet. I live on Don't street, a street that has eyes.
Don't let me catch you, don't get your father, stay out past,
break your grandmother's, don't stare, don't be there
in the first place. Beside trash bins, pigeons cluster and coo.
To have a scar, first there must be a wound, and in some cases,
screams. Danger pulls his car over, finds a parking spot
and waits. To act means to summon authorities, to mind
someone else's business. Kitty Genovese works in a bar,
lives with a woman, walks home from work, calls out
as he slams her into a doorway. She rings the buzzers to get in,
but Everyone covers their ears. The quiet deafening. If teeth
are bricks, the tongue has to be a jackhammer. Blood
on the sidewalk. Photos at 11. What about the last couple,
the ones who had the chance, the ones who could have?
Are their children tucked in, drapes drawn, blinds closed
behind them? It's ten o'clock. Do you know where
your children are?

(ii) *What if*

you spend your whole life thinking that something
really happened, because everyone told you that it
happened, but then you find out that it didn't exactly
happen like that. Take my neighborhood, Kew Gardens,
1964, take the murder of Kitty Genovese, so many years ago
generations passed, most of the witnesses are gone,
and maybe even their grandchildren do not know
what to think. At the Big Park, there is no such thing as time:
the ball still smacks the wall, comes back, smacks the wall
again. They called it *bystander syndrome*, when someone
thinks that others will help so they don't do anything, even
when someone shouts out in pain with her final breath.
Someone will report it, they think, as the theory goes, and
someone did, actually. Someone yelled stop, Robert Mozer,
and temporarily the killer ran away, but when the coast was clear,
he came back. Someone sat with Kitty waiting for the police,
Sophie Farrar. Names not mentioned by the newspapers,
though thirty-eight other people did witness Kitty Genovese
being attacked. To have a syndrome we must have enough
people who do something, or do not do something, then a team
of public policy experts who name what they did or didn't do.
And then it is a syndrome. What if we fail each other,
more times than we know, and in more ways than we know?
What if to speak means to open a wound, a knot of rage and grief?
When a wound heals on a body, it stitches tight, but what if
the scar is over your lips? what if every time you want to speak,
you open it again, would you heal, get quiet, slowly scar over?
What if the ones you love say hush, not now, just hush.
What I mean is that so many did not help and two people
did help. No one recalls the names of those who did.

His Team

This was the baseball team that crackled
into the air while he walked the dog,
took out trash, piled papers. It was the team
that made him rise up in his chair, shout back
at the TV, the team whose fans left before
the 7th-inning stretch, a stiff-legged center fielder,
a guy on first who never reached for a ball,
has-beens, rejects from real teams. It was the team
that broke everybody's hearts. How could anyone love
those losers? The pride of a town where neon signs
skipped letters, sidewalks cracked and curbs crumbled.
Not like that other team, my team, the ones
who showed the world what it meant to win,
year after victorious year. No lost chances, no room
for regrets. Now, I am that kid in the window
and this is how he looks: it is springtime.
He never worries about this foolhardy love of his.
He takes the empty subway home.
He stares the darkness down.

Partners in Crime

When he went out to walk the dog, I slipped him
cigarettes. When I rushed though weekend chores,
he kept mum about my shoddy work. By twelve
I was good enough to be his partner in paddleball.
He had a ferocious serve, set a spin on that dense
black ball. It took off from his paddle, exploded
over the line. I played backcourt and practiced a swing
that (when I got lucky), brought the ball low on the wall,
sent it dribbling back for a kill. Together we defended
the court against all comers, then raced the dark,
straggled in late for supper, swore we lost track
of time, swore it would never happen again.

Changeling

Nothing went according to plan.
It was the way the world
twisted a notch when you entered
through those steel doors

how you learned that books
were written by men whose feats
inspired you to be more, well, manly,
but how those manly feats

weren't suitable for young ladies,
that no matter how well you threw
the ball, the dugout was where
they put the girls, and how

to un-raise your hand, keep
your big ideas to yourself, you knew
the answer, you figured it out
the hard way. And on the bus, a man

waited one step between you
and the exit door, thrust
his finger up your plaid skirt
hard enough to make your stomach

ache, and you did not have the words
to describe that, but you had
to be stupid and powerless
to let that happen. You lost

a bit of wonder every day.
And on the map of you, separate
countries began to form,
distinct borders, one shame

at a time. It did not happen
for two weeks, and then it happened
again. You never asked for help,
you watched the 0's mount up

on the scoreboard, you put on
your game face, squinted down
from the bleachers, decided
surrender was the way to win.

Throwing Like a Girl

It's the grip, the hold,
the reach, the let go
and the follow through,
and still that softball wobbles
like a flapjack, catching the wind
and hanging while the runner
heads for home. There should be
nothing to it — just hurl it,
for crying out loud, blast it—
but that stutter, that hiccup,
all bogged down, like a thought
you tried to force yourself
not to say, or like waking up to find
that men stare in bowling alleys
and on buses, small talk disappears
into excruciating pauses, and you've
grown breasts. They are just there,
like the huge peaches that grew
on Mrs. Rizzo's tree, a scrawny gallows
bent almost double from the weight
of those rose-tinged fruit. It is more
than you wanted and it is less, too,
some part is now missing, and this
new you is not you at all. You need
certainty; now all roads lead to
humiliation, the kind of shame that arcs
back and forth between you and your
body. It cools you down, gets
in the way. You want to be nimble,
you want to mean business. You want
the kind of heat that burns
like a fastball, you want to take
no prisoners, and you will not,
you can bet on it, once you figure out
how to get your own self
back into the game.

The Bird Cage

Shiny lights and triple mirrors.
One for loathing, one for pouting,
one for denial. Sizes are brought.
So many dots and flowers. Imagine
the self-portrait you wanted to paint.
You can almost hear it ripping
into strips. If you wanted to murder someone,
you would never get away with it.
And then, it's time for lunch.

You squeeze into the elevator,
slide the brass grate shut. *Fifth floor,*
says a male voice, *The Bird Cage.*
The shopping bags won't fit under
tiny steel chair legs. The waitress chirps,
but only at your mom. Consider your mom,
specs low on her nose, fumbling for the charge card,
her face a neon sign flashing *Just Behave.*
You see it all, snaring you by the ankles,
dragging you upward into your plastic future.

Which animal does a *fashionista* order?
Veal? Ocelot? Passenger pigeon?
The drinks all have tropical bird names.

Bees

My dog snaps at bees, angles toward them,
following with his nose, nearsightedly inspecting
each bee in a way that would make me nervous
if I was that close, which I almost am,

holding the other end of his leash. More than once
bees have swarmed me as I stumbled onto a hive,
but the first time it was on the shortcut
to Toni Bacon's house; later I realized how huge

the entrance was, a dark cavity on the trail's edge,
bees zeroing in, racing out, an underground society
brimming with danger. Toni's mom applied baking soda
to my arms and neck, soaped the skin on my dusty feet,

checked to see if stingers had lodged. That was the last time
I walked barefoot to Toni's house. I was 12, Toni was 14,
but having an older brother plus going to Catholic school
had made her seem even older. She knew what kind of sin

it was to kiss (actual), to allow a boy to slip his tongue
into your mouth (venial), and to kill someone (mortal),
and most mysterious of all, how confession cleansed
a person's soul, no matter the sin. For about a week,

the welts smarted and swelled; meanwhile we heard
how Georgie Merusi bought an ice-cream pop
from the Good Humor truck at the edge of the beach,
and, taking his first lick, got stung on his tongue.

I pictured this in horror, the angry buzz still in my ears.
Georgie used to tackle me in the water, ducking under,
grabbing my legs from below. I fought back,
but he was as solid as a block wall, a kid whose

hair spiked like a porcupine when his dad
gave him a buzz cut for football practice.
Soon school would start, things would change,
but I remember he held me far enough away

so I could not punch back. Then he stuck out
his tongue, and all I could think about
was how fearless it felt to stare
at that famous tongue, like a gift

just to see it, how bright
it seemed, and how dark the mouth
behind it, his voice asking, "So, what
are you going to do now?"

Playland

I am hiding in the public restroom at Rye Playland
because the world is spinning, is spinning
like a Tilt-a-Whirl, not a Ferris Wheel. The view
from the bathroom is not that elevated. The pattern

on the floor is mostly black and white tiles
in the shape of hexagons, six whites like flower petals
or seats in the Mad Hatter's Tea Cup ride revolving
around a little black hexagon. Surrounded.

This pattern should stand still, but instead,
it contracts and expands like the Hall of Mirrors,
or maybe it is my brain, a disco ball right now,
step right up and party down. What am I thinking?

Everything here is sort of familiar and sort of
shady, like a parallel universe where anything
is possible but also not quite what it seems.
Through the hazy cobwebs on the stall window,

the full moon like a mother, sees it all. Most
of my so-called friends are still on the boardwalk
smoking Camels and drinking Schlitz beer,
though soon enough they may send someone

to check on me. And the floor revolves like
dozens of pretty pinwheels, long drags glowing red
at the tip of menthol cigarettes take my breath away,
warm beer from cans tastes like sweat and boys,

bare bulbs and streetlights turn into sparklers as moths
beat the air with their wings. It is almost the end
of summer, return buses idling in the parking lot. None
of those bus drivers care if I don't get on.

Back from Aqueduct

When he and I walked in the door from that sooty subway track
where the rose vendor's closed barricade said *María te amo*
in double bubble letters, from the no-turning-back
click of twin steel turnstiles, where the cashier with the afro
flicked out tokens from behind the iron grating,
where the only one to meet our eyes was a transit cop
as he ranged from car to car, she would still be up, waiting,
apron on, the sheen of copper pots reflected in the stove top,
each plate back in place, nothing in the drainboard,
every fingerprint scrubbed from the refrigerator door,
and, I can say it now, what is not lost and can't be ignored
is how every bright pan, every spotless counter, was more
than a tactical gamble, it was a vanguard against sin,
a wager against darkness, a bet she needed to win.

Jetstar 88

When the trifecta hit they bought new carpet. They invited everyone over. The new tv fell off a truck. When his picks tanked, he borrowed from everyone, acted like he never missed a paycheck. I wish I could say he never cheated anyone out of anything.

I still see him behind the wheel of a shiny new Oldsmobile, black as night, hubcaps spinning like planets. I wish I could say he stood up for fair play. I wish I could say his hands were not that soft.

That new car smell, Old Spice and soft leather, the way it says luxury, like one mink stole, like one penny on every windowsill, how one thing can erase a lifetime of wait. He died with 21 lottery tickets in his wallet. I wish I could say no one cared about that Jetstar 88, hubcaps spinning like planets.

Blues for Apartment 5G

A mother's pain is a song a house sings.
A woman's body is a vessel for pain.

> Doctors and specialists just can't explain.
> *Hush now, don't explain* sings Billie or Ella.

Her hand is a rosebud, it cups and closes.
Soft tender fingers, blue bruises on roses.

> She spends her days on a blue velvet sofa.
> Stranded and shipwrecked on a blue velvet sea.

Bring her soft food, massage her sore feet.
Please, children, don't cause her more grief.

> *Good morning, heartache,* sings Ella or Billie.
> Each aching lyric swirls silence and sorrow.

Another LP ticks down the spindle.
A mother's pain is the song a house sings.

Mimosa

Wind blows down the avenue, summer
in Queens, everyone's windows open
and you can catch the Yankee game
from every taxi or idling car at a traffic light,
truck exhaust mixing with asphalt, diesel from buses;
the smell says pizza from noon to midnight,
but for some reason, in front of my building
something a little rank, like soaked gym socks,
the spent flowers from a mimosa, which inconveniently
stick onto every parked car's hood, mansard roof, or
windshield wipers. Leggy tree, straining toward
the sun between buildings, in a small square
of dirt cut out of the concrete sidewalk,
marked by dogs, backed into by inept parkers,
scrawny limbs and naked, barkless branches.
Back in July, festooned by pink and white flowers
like little ruffled parasols in a cocktail, it was
as out of place as a movie set prop, a neon
beach umbrella without a beach in sight.
Oh, mimosa. If I ever am so lucky to have a tree,
I used to think, way before I ever had a tree
or drank a mimosa, I would never have one
as skanky as a slit-thigh prom dress, promising
way too much, with touch-me-not leaves that clamp
together when brushed or patted. Not me.
In those days, everything was already impossibly clamped
to everything else. I had no idea who I wanted to be,
but I know what it felt like, moment by moment, to be
surrounded by everything galling. Maybe some other
girl looked out over the fire escape while waiting for a GTO
to double park with its flashers on, radio blasting
"Can't take my eyes off of you," maybe someone
(say my mom) on a beautification committee
would plant a mimosa and hope the block, for one month

in summer, would look like a fairy tale. But now
it's almost September. School's back in session.
The pennant race is heating up. Across the street,
Luigi is dripping sweat and his transom fan blows
hot cheese and tomato sauce out onto the block.
Poor tree, hungry for light, hungry for a tropical breeze,
drops her faded droopy flowers onto every hubcap
and into every storm drain. She can't wait to get away,
but she's a little too desperate to show it.

What We Did

We stayed up all night on the rooftop,
where empty bottles of MD 2020
and tubes of airplane model glue, spent,
lined up in piles next to the pigeon coop
with the small arch shaped windows,
the thick spattered drips of shit running down the bricks,
the soft sleepy coos and clucks of doves
the breeze that carried clouds of soot,
exhaust of diesel buses, and smoking brakes
of delivery trucks from the street below, all that rancid waste
somehow sweetened by the must of feathers and warm tar.

The only reason was because we could,
because our parents were out doing what parents do,
because our learning required that we see the world
from a different perspective, because the neon sign
of the bowling alley down the block and across
the street shone alternately pink and green, and
because the pre-dawn sky was a dingy brown
with the glaze and grit of the streetlights and
the eastern star, and a sliver of a moon hanging.

And on the radio were Diem and Ho, and on the tv
Buddhists set themselves ablaze for peace, but for us
it was nothing but spray paint, red brick and plywood
and how good and bad became confused with each other
in ways we just couldn't reach
or wouldn't have known how to talk about.

And we were sunburned and we were moving
through tunnels beneath buildings, up stairwells,
through the banging steel-hinged door
where warm ooze stuck to our naked feet,
chips of glass and brick mixed with feathers,

and when we looked toward the east
we could almost see the elevated train,
the Jamaica Avenue line, and beyond that, Rockaway,
the ocean and forever, and we could turn the radio up
as loud as we wanted, this house of the rising sun,
this sun that burned through the thin distant haze,
and we spread dirty sheets on that sullied ground,
and after making art, we looked at the sky.

He never said he wanted out

he just stood in the doorway
and waved. Hard to know if he
was coming or going, half
smile on his face, OTB
tickets in his pocket, his
excuses like horses at
the gate, waiting for the bell.

First you dig a pit

my mother calls, my brother sings, my boys
chant, because the sand is warm and soft,
the beach is clearing, lifeguards gone,
and the trunk pops open, out come shovels,
an armful of blankets, a radio, branches
of apple wood or hickory, the lobster pot.

But wait, the pit isn't first. First, mussels
plucked from seaweed on rocks after high tide,
or first, corn bought from Latham's please, or else
it might be mealy, lobsters ordered from that guy,
the same guy as last year, then the pit gets deeper,
someone wraps potatoes in foil, someone crumples
the classifieds, and someone lugs the cooler
with coleslaw, condiments, wine.

The wind picks up, the fire sparks, crackles,
settles into itself, hot enough for a grill grate,
a lobster pot, each part of the meal set in the order
it needs to cook as well as the order it needs
to be eaten. Then the real work starts, bread
yanked in hunks, mussels steamed open,
lobster claws cracked, butter and juices dripping—
where does food stop and the body start?
where does the ocean end and the sky start?
where does the light go? Shimmering tide
sweeps the shoreline, the boys share a blanket,
their bodies outlined in moonlight. In the pit,
the embers glow like molten glass.

Control

Here's my brother, again,
with my father's smile
the one that he flickered on
when he had to, when
he wanted others to
almost like him, say, when he
finally stopped to ask for
directions and made a joke
out of it, *I can speak to them*
in their own language
he'd say, pulling into some
gas station out in the country,
where men wore bib overalls smudged
from labor as strange to him as the roads
that led us to where we
all wished we weren't, and now
that smile shows up, thin
and grim, keeping a lid on
but soon to boil over if some car
in front had left its blinker flashing,
or hung out in the passing lane
but didn't drive fast enough,
or someone honked, *so*
your horn works, now try your
lights, white knuckles on the wheel,
foot on the accelerator, and after
the first time it wasn't
that funny, and now
my brother's body isn't his own,
Dad's uninvited ghost
barges back, not a hint
of regret, no way to know
how to deal with it,
now it's drawing a map

on my brother's lips, that road
between slapstick and slap,
sucker and punch, in control
and out of it.

Behind the Dunes

And here we are again, on this hot blanket
on this scorching sand, under this scorching sun,
while the surf rolls in, rolls in, in silken curls,
each swell rising, rising up the shoreline,
and we've set the large umbrella to shade
our mother's small frame, her silken curls,
her brown arms as thin as driftwood.

She moves slowly now, as if she has
so much time, solar time, the span of the arc
of all these sunlit days, of all of us
in her orbit, drawn to her side. We watch
her eyes close, see that she is, for the moment,
at peace with all the many defeats.
She used to do it all, bike to the beach,
powerwalk the shoreline, swim laps,
everyone had to race to keep up.

These days she relies on our arms
or a cane, and I question the effort it takes
to get her to this blanket near the shore.
Still, we ease her into her chair,
tote the ice chest, food she can barely digest.
We are here, then, when the wind brings
the dank musk of seaweed, and we stay until after
other families pack up, their blankets draging
trails on the sand, their laughter and calls
fading into the flap and cry of gulls.

Off shore, schools of spearing leap,
a sailboat bobs beside a buoy, dark surf
froths along a rocky jetty, but here she is,
under the fluttering umbrella,
the sun melting behind the dunes,

the crook of her fingers holding fast,
and why wouldn't we stay until
all the shadows lengthen, why shouldn't
this last day last long into the night?

Silt and Mystery

Brother, it's my turn. I have dozens of your letters,
each one newsy but also mum, in case eyes

look over my shoulder as I read or as you type,
clacking and dinging on Mom's old Royal, the one

you cleaned and oiled, could not bear to part with.
It wasn't what you wrote, it was the feel

of each page, the dipped "o" and filled-in "a,"
how keys sprung to life under your fingertips.

You tried to fix every broken thing, keep
blood surging through the arteries of the family.

You changed your voice, delivery, became anyone.
It's how you got Mom to laugh, figured out

how to be who you needed to be, to hide
and make believe. You are the one who stayed.

In the photo album of my mind, I see
your hazel eyes flecked with gold, sunburnt nose,

flash of freckles. You were all ears, elbows, feet,
hands three sizes bigger than the rest of you,

a little clumsy. I used to think I was the tough one,
threading live nightcrawlers onto your hook,

clasping a wriggling sunfish until it stilled,
easing a barb from its torn mouth and settling it

back into the lake. We stood on the shoreline,
hoped the spiny dorsal fin would rise,

the tail would swish, that it would dash away
safe and out of sight, into the silt and mystery.

Household Gods

Two weeks after my grandmother died, I dreamt
she lay under my dining room table, arms crossed
over her heart, eyes open, dark and shining. She did
not speak. I was the only one seated, though the table was set
for ten. I'm so glad to see her that my deflated heart
begins to fill with blood and pump again. At the funeral,
her five brothers, icy as separate stones in a field,
tossed clumps of dirt onto her pine box. What silent pleas
could their lips be framing?

When her own mother died, her day starts at sunrise,
walking to a farm, selecting a hen for dinner,
hoping to find an egg inside. The soup pot
steaming spells, the *lares* and *penates*
help her cast a temporary truce. Serving father
then brothers, bussing the table before battles resume.
"Get off your feet, Anne," no one said.

If you google "grenade," you learn you can
put the pin back in, but you must have help
to do it. After the last prayer, the gods fold
their soft wings—all that's left are things,
territory to divide, everyone's hands like clasps
on a steamer trunk, snapping shut. Cracks
became breaks. Back home, I unpacked cups
and plates, a bladed chopper with a maple bowl,
the dust of walnuts in its scored surface, her
chopping pattern in my brain, a clatter and rattle
that my forearm can match. Maybe she can watch,
maybe these are my household gods. I use the plates
every day. I do know she did not give up or give in.
She held on. She did not give up at all.

Her Death

Her death lasts sixteen months
held off by sheer grit and will
she did it for us, you see
we shouldn't have been surprised.

Held off by sheer grit and will
it might have started as a bad dream
we shouldn't have been surprised
her death was a furtive visitor.

Maybe it seemed like a bad dream
slinking in when no one else was there
or maybe a furtive visitor,
a shifting shadow in dim hospital light.

Slinking in when no one else is there
as brazen as a subway rat
a shifty shadow in dim light
like a cousin with bad breath and bad politics.

As brazen as a subway rat
with his hand out, taking, taking
like that cousin no one wants to run into
who manages to get what he wants.

Always has his hand out, taking, taking
hard to embrace him while others watch
still, he knows how to get what he wants
he shuffles and deals, lets her cut the cards.

She won't embrace him while others watch
her death lasts sixteen months
he shuffles and deals, but she cuts the cards.
She did it for us, you see.

Broken Moon

Apartment windows glazed with soot, every darkened room
a grid of panes, a slice of sky, just out of reach, a broken moon

puddles in the blacktop, mirrored by hubcaps, glimpses of infinity
in fractured halos, each streetlight hanging like a token moon

a stalled bus opens its doors at the bus stop, a neon biker
stitches the streets, traffic lights flash like desires unspoken, moon

at dawn, moon at noon, sun flees west, all slides toward dark
we know when the stars will rise, but not you, un-woken moon

if time is distance, and distance is time, then how can we measure
months that fracture into moments, splinters of a broken moon

is it a song that keeps you with me, is that how I still know
the gauze of night, these echoes heard that can't be spoken, moon-

light can hold it all, a song of sorrow in dimming light, how gravity
calls me to the world, but the world still wounds me open, moon.

Notes:

Page 18: "Saved" was inspired by a poem by Camille T. Dungy called, "still in a state of uncreation."

Page 21: Bystander Syndrome: The term "bystander effect" was coined after the brutal murder of Kitty Genovese on March 13, 1964 in Queens, NY. For more information, readers may wish to consult https://www.simplypsychology.org/Kitty-Genovese.html

Page 27: "Lord & Taylor's Bird Cage restaurant and tea room was opened in the late 1930s. It continued on the fifth floor of the Fifth Avenue New York City store until the 1980s. . ." (source: https://restaurant-ingthroughhistory.com/2008/08/07/lunching-in-the-bird-cage/)

Page 48: *Lares and Penates*: In ancient Rome, the *lares and penates* were the protective gods of a household, and they came to be used to signify the home itself. The phrase is generally used to refer to those things that are considered to be the essential elements of someone's home (thefreedictionary.com)

Bonnie Proudfoot was born and raised in Queens, NY. She moved to the Appalachian region in 1979. Her short fiction and poetry have appeared widely in journals. She received a Fellowship for the Arts from the WV Department of Culture and History. Her first novel, *Goshen Road* (Swallow Press, 2020) was longlisted for a PEN/Hemingway Award and recognized by the Women's National Book Association for its 2020 Great Group Reads. *Household Gods* is her first book of poetry. She lives in Athens, Ohio, with her songwriter husband, where she writes and creates artwork in glass.